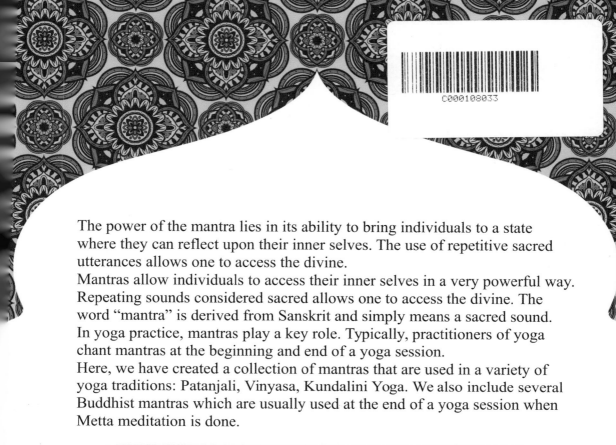

The power of the mantra lies in its ability to bring individuals to a state where they can reflect upon their inner selves. The use of repetitive sacred utterances allows one to access the divine.

Mantras allow individuals to access their inner selves in a very powerful way. Repeating sounds considered sacred allows one to access the divine. The word "mantra" is derived from Sanskrit and simply means a sacred sound. In yoga practice, mantras play a key role. Typically, practitioners of yoga chant mantras at the beginning and end of a yoga session.

Here, we have created a collection of mantras that are used in a variety of yoga traditions: Patanjali, Vinyasa, Kundalini Yoga. We also include several Buddhist mantras which are usually used at the end of a yoga session when Metta meditation is done.

We have added a QR code to all songs. You can follow the link and listen to the rhythm before beginning to play.

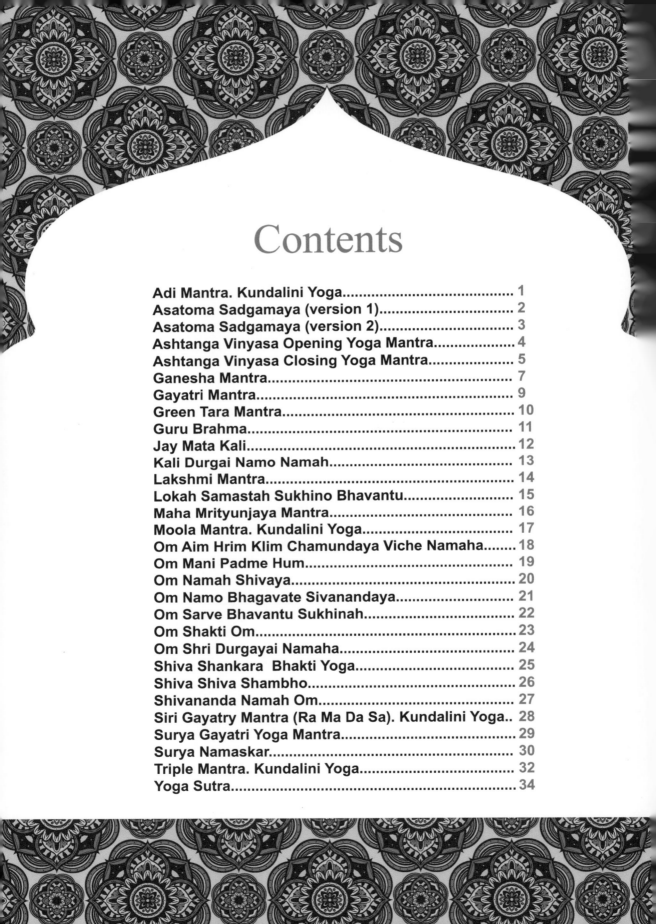

Contents

Adi Mantra

Ong____ Na - mo   Gu - ru - de Na - mo

Ong____ Na - mo - o____   Gu - ru - de Na - mo

Asato Ma Sadgamaya

Version 1

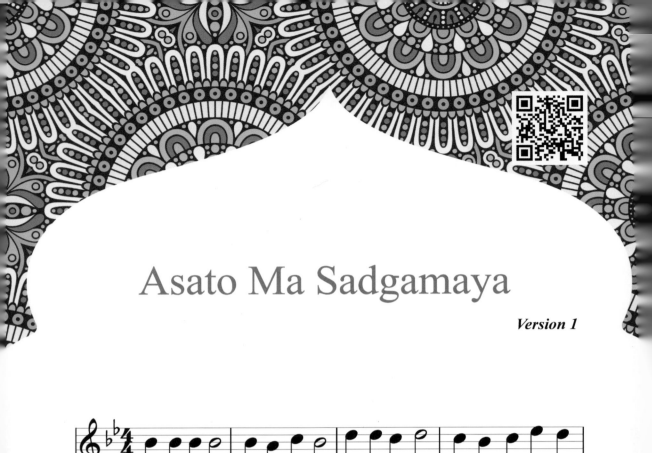

Om Asatoma Sat Gamaya

Version 2

Ashtanga Vinyasa Opening Yoga Mantra

Om   Van - de Guru - nam Cha - ra - na - vin - de

San - dar - shi - ta Svat - ma Su - ka - va Bo - dhe

Nih Sre - ya - se Janga - li - ka - ya - ma - ne

Sam - sa - ra Ha - la - ha - la___ Mo - ha - shan - tyai

A - ba - hu Puru - sha - ka - ram_____

Shan - kha - ca - kr - si Dha - ri - nam_____

Sa - ha - sra Sira - sam_____ Sve - tam

Pra - na - ma - mi Pa - tan - ja - lim

Ashtanga Vinyasa Closing Yoga Mantra

Ganesha Mantra

Om　Gam Ga - na - pa - ta - ye　Na - mo___ Na - ma - ah Shri

Sid - dhi Vi - na - yak - ak　Na - mo___ Na - ma - ah　Ash - ta - vi - na - yak

Na - mo___ Na - ma - ah　Ga - na - pa - ti Bap - pa　Mo - ry - a Om

1.

2.

Mo - ry - a Om　Gam Ga - na - pa - ta - ye　Na - mo___ Na - ma - ah Shri

Sid - dhi Vi - na - yak - ak   Na - mo___ Na - ma - ah

Ash - ta - vi - na - yak - ak   Na - mo___ Na - ma - ah

Ga - na - pa - ti Bap - pa   Mo - ry - a Om   Mo - ry - a

Gayatri Mantra
(Savitri Mantra)

Om Bhur Bhu-vah Sv - ha Tat Sa - vi -

tur____ Va - re - ny - am_____ Bhar - go De -vas-ya

Dhi - ma hi Di - yo Yo - nah_____ Pra - cho - da - yat

Green Tara Mantra

Guru Brahma

Jay Mata Kali

Kali Durga Namo Namah

Ka - li Dur - ga Na - mo Na - ma - a - ah

Ka - li Dur - ga Na - mo Na - mah

Lakshmi Mantra

Om Shrim Ma - ha   Lak - shmi - yay Swa - ha

14

Lokah Samastah Sukhino Bhavantu

Lo - ka_____ Sa - mas - tah_____ Suk - hi -

no _____ Bha - van - tu_____

Maha Mrityunjaya Mantra

Moola Mantra

Ha - ri Om___ Tat Sat   Ha - ri   Om   Tat Sat

Om Aim Hrim Klim Chamundaye Viche Namaha

Rubato

Om   Aim   Hrim   Klim   Cha - mun - da - ye   Vi - che

Om Mani Padme Hum

Om Namah Shivaya

Om Namo Bhagavate Sivanandaya

Om Na - mo Bha -ga - va - te Si - va - na - da - ya

Om Sarve Bhavantu Sukhinah

Om Sar - ve Bha - van - tu Su - khi - na - ah Sar - ve San - tu Ni -

ra - ama - yaah Sar - ve - e Bha - dra - anni Pa - shyan - tu

Ma Ka - schid Duh - ka Bhaag Bha - vet____

Om Shan - ti - ih Shan - ti - ih Shan - ti - ih

22

Om Shakti Om

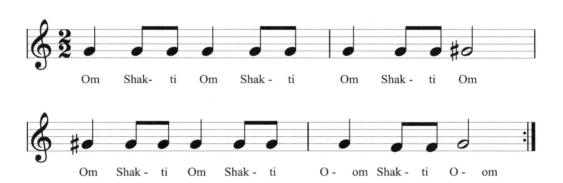

Om   Shak- ti Om   Shak - ti   Om   Shak - ti Om

Om   Shak - ti Om Shak - ti   O - om Shak - ti O - om

Om Shri Durgayai Namaha

Om Shri Dur - ga - yai Na ma ha

Shiva Shankara

Ja - ya Shi - va   Shan - ka- ra   Bham Bham Ha-ra Ha-ra

Ha-ra   Ha-ra   Ha-ra   Ha-ra   Ha - ra   Bol Ha - re

Shiva Shiva Shambho

Shivananda Namah Om

Shi - va - nan - da Na - mah Om   Ja - ya Gu - ru - de - ev

Om Gu - ru Ja - ya Gu - ru   De Va - ya   Om Gu - ru Ja - ya Gu - ru

Ja - ya Gu - ru - de - ev   Om Gu - ru Ja - ya Gu - ru   De Va - ya

27

Siri Gayatry Mantra
(Ra Ma Da Sa)

Surya Gayatri Yoga Mantra

Om   A - di - tya - ya Vid - ma - he_____

Mar - tan - da - ya Dhi - ma - hi_____

Tan - nah Sur - ya   Pra - co - da - yat

Surya Namaskar

Triple Mantra.
Kundalini Yoga

Aad Gu - ray Na - meh____ Jud - gad Gu - ray Na - meh

Sat Gu - ray Na - meh Si - ri Gu - ru Day - vay Na - meh Aad Sa - ch Jud - gaad Sach

Hai Bhee Sach Na - na - k Ho - see Bhee Sach Aad Sa - ch - Jud - gad Sach Hai Bhee Sach

Na - na - k Ho - see Bhee Sach Aad Gu - ray Na - meh____ Jud -

Yoga Sutra

Printed in Great Britain
by Amazon

40115964R00023